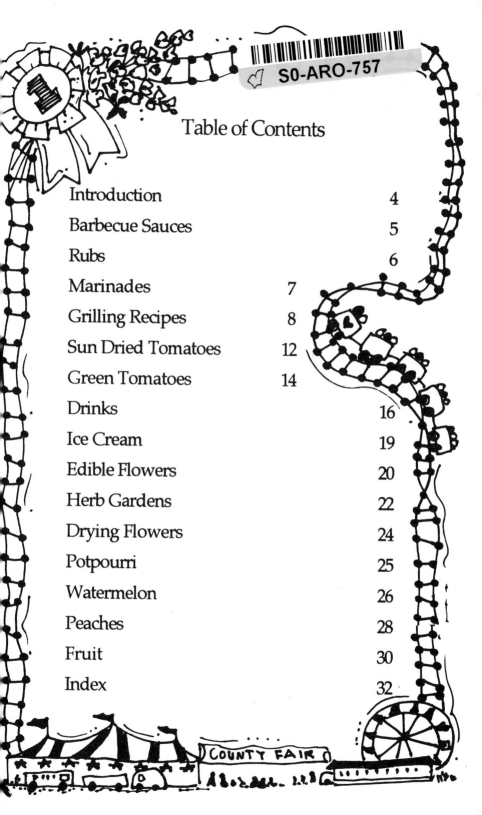

Table of Contents

COUNTY FAIR

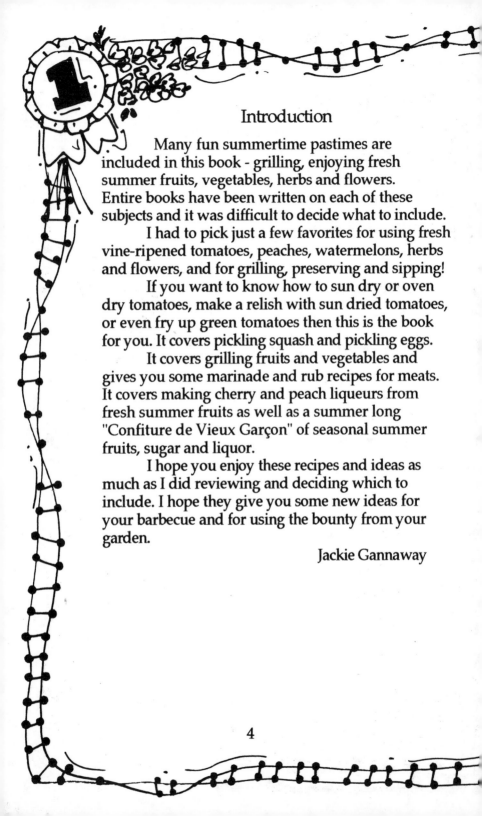

Introduction

Many fun summertime pastimes are included in this book - grilling, enjoying fresh summer fruits, vegetables, herbs and flowers. Entire books have been written on each of these subjects and it was difficult to decide what to include.

I had to pick just a few favorites for using fresh vine-ripened tomatoes, peaches, watermelons, herbs and flowers, and for grilling, preserving and sipping!

If you want to know how to sun dry or oven dry tomatoes, make a relish with sun dried tomatoes, or even fry up green tomatoes then this is the book for you. It covers pickling squash and pickling eggs.

It covers grilling fruits and vegetables and gives you some marinade and rub recipes for meats. It covers making cherry and peach liqueurs from fresh summer fruits as well as a summer long "Confiture de Vieux Garçon" of seasonal summer fruits, sugar and liquor.

I hope you enjoy these recipes and ideas as much as I did reviewing and deciding which to include. I hope they give you some new ideas for your barbecue and for using the bounty from your garden.

Jackie Gannaway

Summertime

Recipes and Crafts

Jackie Gannaway

COUNTY FAIR

Published in Austin, TX by COOKBOOK CUPBOARD, P.O. Box 50053, Austin, TX 78763 (512) 477-7070

ISBN 0-885597-05-3

Artwork by Mosey 'N Me   1436 Baird   Katy, Texas 77493   (713) 391-2281

Mail Order Information

To order a copy of this book send a check for $3.95 + $1.50 for shipping (TX residents add 8 % sales tax) to Cookbook Cupboard, P.O. Box 50053, Austin, TX 78763. Send a note asking for this title by name. If you would like a descriptive list of all the fun titles in The Kitchen Crafts Collection, send a note asking for an order blank. One title that fits in with summertime is "Watermelon Days" - over 40 watermelon recipes. The watermelon recipes in this book came from "Watermelon Days". All the Kitchen Crafts titles are $3.95.

Barbecue Sauces

Never add barbecue sauce until the last 20 minutes of cooking. The sugar in the sauce will caramelize and burn.

Ginger Barbecue Sauce

3/4 cup dark corn syrup
1/2 cup catsup

1/4 cup Worcestershire sauce
1/4 cup mustard
2 tsp. ground ginger

Place all ingredients in medium bowl. Blend with whisk. Store in refrigerator.

Asian Barbecue Sauce

1 cup soy sauce
1/4 cup sherry
2 Tb. peeled and chopped
   fresh gingerroot

1 tsp. chopped garlic (from jar)
3/4 cup frozen apple juice con-
   centrate, thawed
3 Tb. sesame oil

Place all ingredients except sesame oil in a medium pan and bring to a simmer. Cook uncovered for 10 minutes. Remove from heat and stir in sesame oil.

Chutney Barbecue Sauce

1/2 cup chutney, chopped
   in food processor
2/3 cup catsup
2/3 cup steak sauce

2/3 cup chili sauce
1/2 cup Worcestershire sauce
1/2 tsp. hot pepper sauce

Place all ingredients in a large bowl. Blend with whisk. Store in refrigerator.

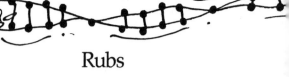

Rubs

Rubs are blends of herbs and spices that give flavor to grilled meat. If the meat is too bulky to marinate, a rub is a good alternative. You can also sprinkle the rub on as a seasoning. To use as a rub, sprinkle generously over the meat and rub in it well before cooking.

To mix all of these rubs, place all ingredients in a medium bowl and blend well with a whisk. Keep extra rub refrigerated.

3 Ingredient Rub

1/2 cup garlic powder   1/2 cup paprika
1/2 cup pepper

Cajun Rub

2 tsp. garlic powder   1 tsp. cayenne pepper
2 tsp. onion powder   1 tsp. pepper
2 tsp. paprika   1 tsp. ground oregano
1 tsp. ground thyme   1/2 tsp. chili powder

Rub for Chicken or Fish

2 Tb. sugar   2 tsp. coarse black pepper
1 Tb. onion powder   2 tsp. cayenne pepper
1 Tb. ground thyme   3/4 tsp. nutmeg
2 tsp. ground allspice   1/4 tsp. ground cloves

Herb Rub for Chicken, Fish or Pork

1 Tb. dried leaf thyme   1 tsp. dried leaf marjoram
1 Tb. dried leaf oregano   1 tsp. dried leaf basil
1 tsp. poultry seasoning   1 tsp. dried parsley flakes
1 tsp. dried leaf rosemary

Marinades

Marinades can flavor and/or tenderize fish, chicken, beef or pork.

Place the food to be marinated in a glass or ceramic dish or a large freezer bag. Prick it with a fork to allow the marinade to soak in. Turn the food over in the marinade several times while marinating.

Allow 1/3 to 1/2 cup marinade for each pound of meat. Save some of the marinade to use for basting. Don't baste with the same marinade used for marinating.

Always marinate in the refrigerator. Marinate for 30 minutes to 6 hours. Fish can marinate 30 minutes. Tough cuts of beef need 6 hours. There are many interesting bottled marinades available.

Honey Lemon Marinade

1/3 cup lemon juice	3 Tb. soy sauce
1/3 cup honey	1 tsp. brown sugar
1 tsp. chopped garlic (from jar)	

Mix all ingredients. Cover and store in refrigerator.

Oriental Marinade

2 Tb. peeled, finely chopped gingerroot	1 1/2 cups orange juice
	1/3 cup sherry
1/3 cup low sodium soy sauce	1/4 cup packed brown sugar
1 tsp. chopped garlic (from a jar)	
1 1/2 tsp. coarse ground pepper	1/2 tsp. ground cumin

Mix all ingredients. Cover and store in refrigerator.

Bourbon Grilled Steak

1 2" thick 2 1/2 lb. sirloin
2 tsp. Worcestershire sauce
1/3 cup bourbon
1/2 cup water

2 Tb. lemon juice
1/2 cup low sodium soy
  sauce
1/3 cup brown sugar

Place steak in a shallow glass or ceramic dish. Mix remaining ingredients and pour over meat, reserving 1/3 cup for basting. Marinate in refrigerator for 4 hours. Baste with reserved marinade while grilling.

Grilled Chicken with Jalapeno Jelly

1/8 tsp. salt
1/4 tsp. coarse pepper
4 chicken breasts

1 cup jalapeno jelly
1 cup white wine
1/4 cup chopped fresh basil

Season chicken with salt and pepper. Combine remaining ingredients in a small pan. Heat over low heat. Reserve half the marinade for basting. Marinate chicken in remaining marinade in refrigerator for 30 minutes. Baste with reserved marinade while grilling.

Grilled Shrimp

1 stick butter, melted
1 Tb. chili powder
1/4 tsp. garlic powder

1 lb. medium shrimp, peeled
  and deveined
bacon slices

Mix first three ingredients in small flat dish. Coat shrimp on both sides in melted butter. Wrap in 1/4 slice bacon. Place in a grilling basket. Grill 5 minutes on each side. For a change, cut the bacon in half. Enclose 1 shrimp and one raw oyster with the bacon half. Secure with a toothpick that has been soaked in water.

Grilled Oysters

1 stick butter, melted
1 small onion, finely chopped
2 tsp. chopped garlic (from jar)

1 tsp. lemon pepper
2 Tb. chopped parsley
24 large raw oysters

Combine all ingredients except oysters in medium bowl. Mix well. Divide mixture among 24 muffin cups. Place oyster in each muffin cup. Place muffin tins on hot grill. Cook 5 to 10 minutes until oysters turn white and edges begin to curl.

Chicken on a Can of Beer

Place a whole chicken over a full, opened can of beer on the grill. (Set the chicken cavity over the can.) Cover and cook as you would any whole chicken. The evaporating beer adds a new, different flavor. You can baste with any sauce you would normally use.

Basting with Herbs

Gather a large handful of fresh sage, parsley, basil, rosemary, parsley or a combination. Tie to a wooden spoon by wrapping with sisal string. Dip in olive oil and baste the chicken, seafood or pork you are grilling. When it is nearly cooked, untie herbs and add to coals for a wonderful aroma.

Grilled Brie

1 (4 oz.) round Brie
3 Tb. packed brown sugar

1 tart apple, cored

Cut Brie in half horizontally to form 2 circles. Sprinkle rough side of Brie with brown sugar. Cut into quarters Cut apple into 16 thin wedges. Place an apple wedge on top of brown sugar. Place wedges on a sheet of heavy duty foil on a grill. Cook covered 5 minutes or until cheese softens and sugar begins to melt. Remove with a spatula.

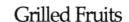

Grilled Fruits

Prepare fruits as directed below. Brush with melted butter or olive oil. (Chopped fresh mint is a good addition.) Place in a grilling basket. Grill, turning often, until fruit is just beginning to brown.

Apples: Core and slice into rings. Grill about 6 minutes.

Bananas: Leave skin on and slice in half lengthwise. Grill about 2 minutes.

Cantaloupe or honeydew: Peel, remove seeds and cut into rings. Grill about 3 minutes.

Figs: Cut in half lengthwise. Grill about 4 minutes.

Pineapple: Peel, core and cut into rings. Grill about 6 minutes.

Grilled Vegetables

Place chunks of eggplant, onions, peppers, zucchini, yellow squash on a metal skewer (or a bamboo skewer which has been soaked in water). Baste with a purchased garlic-herb-olive oil marinade.

Sliced vegetables can also be marinated and placed in a grilling basket to grill.

Grilled Corn

Peel back the husks of the corn, leaving them attached. Remove the silks. Rinse the corn and soak the husks. Brush corn with melted butter.

At this point, you can choose a seasoning:
1. Squeeze generously with fresh lime juice and sprinkle lightly with black pepper
2. Add finely chopped red bell pepper.
3. Season each ear with 1/4 tsp. chopped fresh rosemary.

Pull the husks back in place and grill 15 to 20 minutes, turning occasionally or bake at 500 for 20 minutes.

Cilantro Lime Butter

1 stick butter, softened   1 Tb. fresh lime juice
2 Tb. chopped cilantro   1/8 tsp. cayenne pepper

Mix all ingredients well. Spread on grilled corn and other grilled vegetables.

Onions on the Pit

Peel large Vidalia or 1015 onions. Cut a small slice from the top of each onion. Cut a criss cross pattern across the top of each onion. Place 1 tsp. butter on top of each onion. Sprinkle lightly with salt, pepper and optional paprika. Wrap onions individually in heavy duty foil. Place on grill cut side up for 30 to 40 minutes.

Cilantro Stuffed Eggs

Process egg yolks in food processor with mayo, sour cream, fresh lime juice, salt, pepper, fresh cilantro and fresh parsley. Fill egg halves. Garnish with a cilantro leaf. Cover and refrigerate up to 1 hour before serving.

Pickled Eggs

2 large jars banana peppers   1 large white onion, chopped
1 quart white vinegar   into chunks
24 to 36 hard boiled eggs,   salt
    peeled   pepper

Combine all ingredients in a large glass container. Cover and let stand 24 or 48 hours. Can add pieces of carrots and cauliflower and cilantro leaves. Refrigerate. Add more eggs as they are eaten and keep it going all summer.

11

Sun Dried Tomatoes

Drying tomatoes intensifies their flavor. Use vine ripened for best flavor. All tomatoes can be dried, even cherry tomatoes. Start with firm tomatoes.

Cut large tomatoes in thin slices. Cut cherry and small tomatoes in half. Cover an oven rack with cheesecloth. Lay tomatoes in single layer on cheesecloth. Cover tomatoes with another layer of cheesecloth.

Place outside in full sun, with good air circulation, for 2 to 3 days. Bring in at night. Takes 5 to 6 days in partial sun. They are ready when dark, dry and shriveled, but still bendable.

If you want them oil-packed, place in dry, sterilized jars. Add fresh basil leaves or sprigs of rosemary, if desired. Cover with virgin olive oil. Cover tightly and store at room temperature. Wait 1 to 4 weeks before using. Add to salads. Make the relish on facing page.

If you don't want them oil-packed, store loosely in paper bags and keep in a dark place for several weeks. After that you can string them and hang away from direct sunlight or place in dry sterilized jars with tight lids. To use tomatoes that are not oil packed, cover with boiling water and allow to soften. Drain and use in salads, spaghetti sauces, pizza or breads

Oven Dried Tomatoes

Place tomato slices on cake racks, not touching. (If cherry tomatoes are used, place cut sides up.) Place cake racks in jelly roll pans. Sprinkle lightly with salt. Place in 200 degree oven. With a gas oven leave them in for 8 hours. With an electric oven, heat for 6 hours in the afternoon, turn off oven and leave overnight. In the morning heat 1 more hour.

Pack and store as described above. These make a good gift. They will keep until Christmas. Add fresh herbs and garlic before giving, for good color.

Sun Dried Tomato Relish

1 cup chopped sun dried
    tomatoes in oil
1/2 cup finely chopped green
    bell pepper
2 cups frozen whole kernel
    corn, thawed
1/2 cup chopped red onion

1/4 cup chopped tomatillos
2 Tb. finely chopped cilantro
1 Tb. finely chopped parsley
2 Tb. fresh lime juice
1 Tb. virgin olive oil
1/2 tsp. finely chopped fresh
    jalapeno
salt and pepper to taste

Mix all ingredients in large bowl. Place in hot, dry, sterilized jars. Seal in hot water bath or store in refrigerator.

Tomato Jam

2 cinnamon sticks, broken
1/2 tsp. whole allspice
1 tsp. whole cloves
1/8 tsp. grated fresh nutmeg

4 1/2 lbs. vine ripened tom-
    atoes, peeled and quartered
4 1/2 cups sugar
1 1/2 cups cider vinegar
5 drops hot pepper sauce

Tie spices in a cheesecloth bag. Place all ingredients in a non aluminum pan. Bring to a boil over medium heat. Lower heat and simmer slowly over medium low heat, stirring frequently until thick. This may take several hours. Discard spice bag. Spoon jam into dry, sterilized jars. Seal and process in hot water bath or store in refrigerator.

Fried Green Tomatoes

Green tomatoes are tomatoes that haven't ripened. They haven't turned red yet. Pick them off your tomato plants when they are green and fry them up. There are two basic ways to fry tomatoes:

Beat 1 egg with 1 Tb. milk in a small bowl,
Mix equal parts cornmeal and flour and place on a saucer.
Slice green tomatoes into 1/4" to 1/2" thick slices.
Dip tomato slices in egg mixture and then coat both sides in flour mixture. Let stand a few minutes before frying.

At this point, either:
Pan fry them in bacon drippings over medium heat until golden brown. Season with salt and pepper.
or:
Deep fry them in a deep fryer or in 1 1/2" of hot vegetable oil.

Green Tomato Relish

5 cups green tomatoes, seeded	1 cup chopped onions
4 cups sugar	1 red bell pepper, chopped
5 cups vinegar	1 green bell pepper, chopped
3 cups chopped cabbage	1/2 cup salt
2 cups chopped celery	1 Tb. pepper

Mix all ingredients in your largest pot. Bring to a boil over medium heat. Turn heat to low and simmer, covered 2 hours and 15 minutes. Have hot, dry, sterilized canning jars ready. Fill jars one at a time with hot relish. Wipe the rim well. Seal and process in hot water bath or store in refrigerator.

Corn Relish

2 (16 oz.) bags frozen whole
    kernel corn, thawed
1 qt. vine-ripened tomatoes,
    chopped
1 1/4 cups sugar
1 qt. chopped onions

2 cups cider vinegar
1/4 cup salt
1 red bell pepper, chopped
2 tsp. celery seed
2 tsp. mustard seed

Mix all in large pot. Bring to boil over medium heat.
Lower heat and simmer 40 minutes. Place hot relish in
dry, sterilized jars. Seal in hot water bath or store in refrigerator.

Sweet Onion Butter

2 sticks butter or margarine,
    softened
1/2 cup grated 1015 or Vidalia
    onions, undrained

2 Tb. minced fresh parsley
2 tsp. pepper
1 tsp. dry mustard

Mix all ingredients on low speed with electric mixer
until well blended. Serve on French bread or baked potatoes.

Pickled Squash

1 gallon yellow squash,
    sliced paper thin
8 small white onions,
    chopped thin
1 green bell pepper, chopped
1 red bell pepper, chopped
1/2 cup ice cream salt

5 cups sugar
1/2 tsp. turmeric
1/2 tsp. ground cloves
2 Tb. mustard seed
2 Tb. celery seed
5 cups white vinegar

Layer squash, onions and peppers in large pot. Cover
with salt and fill with ice and water. Cover and set aside 3
hours. Combine remaining ingredients in large pan and
bring to a boil. Drain squash and place pot on stove. Pour hot
vinegar over squash. Bring back to a boil. Stir well. Spoon
immediately into hot, dry, sterilized jars. Seal. Store in refrigerator.

Spiced Sun Tea

1 gallon cold water	1 tsp. whole cloves
3" cinnamon stick, broken	8 tea bags

Place water in a gallon glass jar with lid. Tie spices in a coffee filter using cotton string. Add tea bags and spice bag to jar. Put on lid and let jar stand in full sun for 8 hours or until it is the strength you like. Remove tea bags and spice bags and discard. Serve with ice, sugar and lemon.

Mint Ice Tea

7 tea bags	juice of 7 lemons
12 sprigs mint	2 cups sugar
peel of 3 lemons	8 cups water
8 cups boiling water	

Steep tea, mint and lemon rind in boiling water for 12 minutes. Remove from water. Add juice and sugar. Stir until sugar dissolves. Strain. Add cold water. Makes 1 gallon.

Mint Ice Cubes

Fill ice cubes trays half full of water. Place a mint leaf in each one and freeze. Finish filling with water and freeze. Serve in ice tea.

Fresh Herb Ice Tea

1 Tb. chopped fresh lemon balm
1 Tb. chopped fresh spearmint
1 Tb. chopped fresh lemongrass
1 cup boiling water

Combine herbs and steep in boiling water for 5 minutes. Strain. Cool to room temperature. Serve over ice. Serves 2.

Red Buds

Chambord liqueur   fresh raspberries
chilled Champagne

 Place 1 raspberry in Champagne flute. Add 2 Tb. Chambord and top with chilled Champagne. Serve immediately.

Red Buds Deluxe

1 (16 oz.) can raspberries Chambord liqueur
 in heavy syrup   chilled Champagne

 Divide raspberries and syrup among ice cube trays and freeze. Place 1 frozen raspberry cube in each Champagne glass. Add 1 Tb. Chambord and top of with Champagne. Serve immediately.

Mimosas

 Mix equal parts chilled Champagne and chilled orange juice. Serve over a raspberry or strawberry in Champagne glass.

Strawberry Mimosas

2 1/2 cups chilled orange juice 1 bottle chilled
1 (10 oz.) box frozen straw-   champagne
 berries, partially thawed

 Puree orange juice and strawberries in blender or food processor. Mix gently with Champagne in a pitcher. Serve immediately in stemmed glasses.

White Wine Special

 Drop a fresh raspberry, strawberry or even a rose petal (pesticide free, of course) into each wine glass before filling with wine or Champagne.

Peach Liqueur

firm fresh peaches
vodka

1/2 cup water
3/4 cup sugar
1 vanilla bean
1 tsp. cinnamon

Wash, dry and quarter peaches with skin. Crack the peach pits by wrapping in a dish cloth and hitting with a hammer. Place peaches and cracked pits in a dry, sterilized quart jar. Fill jar with peaches and pits. Cover with vodka. Let stand 2 weeks in a cool dark place.

Mix water, sugar, vanilla bean and cinnamon in small pan. Simmer 5 minutes. Cool. Strain liquid through cheesecloth in a strainer. Stir sugar syrup into strained peach liquid. Cover and let stand 2 months in a cool, dark place.

Cherry Liqueur

1 lb. fresh sweet cherries
   with stems, not too ripe

3/4 cup sugar
vodka

Place cherries in a dry, sterilized quart jar. Sprinkle evenly with sugar. Fill jar with vodka. Put on lid. Let stand 2 months in a cool dark place. Serve in little cups. Put 2 - 3 of the cherries with stems in the cup to eat.

Do the same with hulled firm fresh strawberries or fresh raspberries. Wash this fruit first and pat until dry. Strain and discard fruit after aging time.

Flowerpot Ice Cream

ice cream
small clay flowerpots

Oreo cookies, crushed
straws, flowers, gummi
worms

Line individual serving size flowerpots with foil. Fill 2/3 full with ice cream. Pack ice cream down. Top with crushed cookie crumbs for "dirt". Wrap in plastic wrap and place in freezer until ready to serve. Place a section of plastic drinking straw into ice cream. At serving time, insert flowers into straw. Decorate with gummi worms. You can do this with a large flowerpot and scoop out the servings from it.

Sorbet in a Lemon

purchased lemon sorbet

fresh lemons
mint or lemon leaves

Cut a 1" long piece off top of lemon. Scoop out all lemon pulp from the lemon and from the piece you cut off. Cut a thin slice off bottom of lemon so it will stand up. Fill lemon with sorbet, mounding up over the top. Wrap in plastic wrap and place in freezer until firm. To serve, top with the 1" piece of lemon (like a little hat). Stick a lemon or mint leaf into the sorbet for garnish.

Can do this in a tangerine with orange sorbet. Can cut a large orange in half and zig zag the edges and fill with sorbet.

Ice Cream Sandwiches

Make your own ice cream sandwiches with oversize chocolate chip cookies and your favorite flavor of ice cream. Wrap in plastic wrap and store in freezer until firm. For prolonged storage place in plastic freezer bags.

Edible Flowers

Many supermarkets sell edible flowers in little cello boxes by the fresh herbs. Certain varieties of flowers are edible and they must be pesticide free.

Growing Edible Flowers

Plant these perennials:
violets, pansies, chives
lemon thyme, lavender
anise hyssop, hyssop
bee balm, winter savory

Plant these annuals:
calendula
nasturtiums
borage
pineapple sage

Plant in full sun. Fertilize every 3 to 4 weeks and cut flowers frequently to keep blooming. The perennials will bloom better after the first year.

Candied Rose Petals

3 egg whites
1 cup superfine sugar

24 fresh rose petals (pesticide-free)

Beat egg whites with whisk until frothy. Place petals on a wax paper lined baking sheet. Put sugar into a small dish. Paint egg white on front and back of a petal using a small paint brush (don't use same brush for paint and food - have a kitchen paint brush).

Place coated rose petal into dish of sugar. Gently spoon sugar over it. Carefully pick up petal with tweezers and shake off excess sugar. Place on waxed paper. Repeat until all petals are sugared. (Beat egg whites again if necessary.)

Let petals stand overnight. When thoroughly dry, place in a jar or bag and store in a cool, dry place.

This can be done to violets, pansies, nasturtiums or any edible flower. Use to decorate a cake or cupcakes. Serve on a try of assorted fruits and cheeses.

Brie with Flowers

2 cups dry white wine	1 pkg. edible flowers
1 envelope unflavored gelatin	1 round Brie cheese, chilled

Mix wine and gelatin in a small pan. Blend well. Let stand 5 minutes. Heat, over medium heat, stirring constantly until gelatin is dissolved and mixture is clear. Place pan into a bowl of ice cubes and water. Stir aspic occasionally (very gently) until it is the consistency of thick syrup. (If it becomes too thick, reheat.)

Place cheese on a cake rack over a jelly roll pan (to catch drips). Arrange flowers on top of Brie in an artistic arrangement. Press flowers flat. Spoon aspic evenly over top and sides of Brie. Let stand at room temperature 3 minutes. Refrigerate. You may need a second coat of aspic after first one has set.

Prepare this the day ahead or in the morning. Place on a plate and cover with a bowl to protect it. Chill until serving time. (Don't put plastic wrap on this.) This recipe makes enough aspic to do 1 large Brie or 2 medium size ones.

Edible Flowers in Salad

red lettuce	1/4 - 1/2 tsp. mustard
curly leaf endive	coarse ground pepper
1 park balsamic vinegar	parsley
3 parts light olive oil	edible flowers
1/4 - 1/2 tsp. chopped garlic	

Wash, dry and tear lettuce. Mix in a salad bowl. Mix vinegar, oil, garlic, mustard and pepper. Pour over lettuce. Toss well and top with chopped parsley and flowers.

Strawberry Pot Herb Gardens

A strawberry pot is a clay flowerpot with holes in the sides. It was designed for planting strawberries so they could trail down the sides.

Fill half way with a good soil mix. Purchase a length of 2" PVC pipe a few inches shorter than your pot. Have 5/8" diameter holes drilled on all sides every 6". Put this in the pot at a slant. Finish filling the pot with soil.

Select herbs in 2" pots. Plant the herb plants in each of the side holes. (Plant the trailing varieties in the sides.)

Plant several different herb plants in the top of the pot. Good choices for full sun are chamomile, basil, dill and fennel in the top of the pot. Mint, parsley, chives, thyme and marjoram are good in the side openings. When planting the sides, add extra soil and pack tightly.

Water the finished garden through the PVC pipe.

Salad Garden

Plant a strawberry pot "salad" garden for the shade. Put romaine lettuce in the top opening and bibb and baby red lettuce in the side openings.

Salsa Garden

Plant a strawberry pot "salsa" garden for the sun. Put tomatoes in top and jalapenos, green peppers, garlic, chives and cilantro in the side openings.

Pasta Garden

Plant a strawberry pot "pasta" garden for the sun. Put basil and oregano in the top and thyme, marjoram and parsley in the side openings.

Living Herb Wreath

You need 2 sizes of wire wreath forms, one that will fit inside the other. Place a layer of wet moss in the larger wreath form. Add potting soil.

Arrange small pots of herbs around the wreath form, allowing room for the plants to grow. Remove the herb plants from their pots and trim 1" of soil off them so they will fit in the wreath frame. Press into place in the wreath.

Place the smaller wreath form in place, gently feeding the herbs plants through the openings in the smaller frame. Wire the two frames together. Fill in with dirt around the plants and press in securely.

Water this by misting daily. Hang in the sun. Cut herbs frequently to use and to keep the plants from getting leggy.

Herb Bath Sachets

1/4 cup rose petals
1/4 cup lavender flowers
1/2 cup rolled oats (for bulk)
3 bay leaves, broken

2 Tb. cut orange peel
2 Tb. cut lemon peel
2 rosemary sprigs, crushed

Mix all ingredients in a large bowl. Blend well. Divide mixture among 4 to 6 small muslin bags. (Make the bags by deciding on the size, sewing around 3 sides, turning right side out and pinking the top edge.) Fill bags with herbs.

Tie closed with a decorative cord or ribbon with long streamers. Use the streamers to hold bag while you swish it in hot bath water. Hang bag from faucet between uses. Each bag is good for 3 to 4 baths.

Good herbs for the bath are peppermint leaves, calendula, rosemary.

Drying Flowers

Cornmeal - Borax Method:

Use the cardboard box that a case of soft drinks comes in. Tape the corners shut securely. Fill box with a mixture of 10 parts white cornmeal to 3 parts Borax (grocery store with the laundry detergents).

Place flowers in mixture. (Pick flowers to dry early in the morning as soon as they open and after dew has dried.) Lay flower heads face up. Gently spoon mixture over flowers. Leave them covered in mixture for 3 to 4 days. Gently pour off mixture. Clean petals with dry paintbrush.

Silica Gel Method:

Place silica gel (crafts store) into a large airtight plastic container with a lid. Lay flower heads face up in mixture. Gently spoon mixture over, around and under flowers. Seal container with lid. Check after 2 to 3 days. Gently pour off crystals. Clean petals with dry paintbrush.

Air Drying Method

Dry whole flowers with leaves and stems this way. Pick early in the morning, after dew has dried. Pick when the bloom is open and full, but not too full

Tie the stems together with a rubber band. Hang upside down in a light, airy place, but not in direct sunlight.

It takes about 1 week to dry, depending on the flower and the humidity.

Roses dry well. They dry darker. Don't start with red roses. Larkspur, delphinium and sunflowers also dry well.

Hydrangeas make good dried flowers, but they need to be left on the plant to dry.

When flowers are dry, spray with hair spray.

Potpourri

To make potpourri, mix dried flower petals, dried herbs, dried citrus peel, whole spices, floral oils and a fixative (cut orris root - get at large nursery or craft store).

Lay petals on an old window screen covered with a piece of cheesecloth. Place in dark room, Stir every few days. You can also spread them on a sheet on the floor of a dark room.

When dry, store in closed bags in a dark closet.

To dry fresh citrus peel, place pieces on a paper plate, not touching. Microwave on high for 2 to 3 minutes, rotating plate 1/2 turn after each minute.

Basic Potpourri Recipe

1 qt. dried flower petals
1 cup dried mixed herb leaves
1 Tb. whole spices (cinnamon
  stick, cloves, allspice,
  cracked nutmeg)
1 Tb. crushed herb seeds
  (anise seed, coriander seed,
  caraway seed)

2 Tb. dried citrus peel
10 drops rose oil
3 drops patchouli oil
5 drops orange oil
3 drops honeysuckle oil
1/4 cup cut orris root (a
  fixative)

Mix all except oils and fixative in a large glass jar with a screw on lid. Place orris root in a small dish and mix in the oils. Add this gently to potpourri. Put on lid and leave in a dark room for 5 to 6 weeks. Stir every 5 days or so.

Pressing Flowers

Pick colorful flowers (wild flowers are perfect) and press between pages of a thick paper back book. Add flowers all summer. Keep book weighted down under a heavy weight. In the winter, put pressed flowers inside notes you are mailing. You can also glue the flowers to heavy white paper and frame under glass.

25

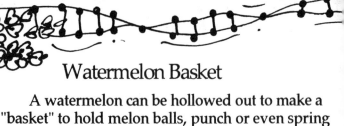

Watermelon Basket

A watermelon can be hollowed out to make a "basket" to hold melon balls, punch or even spring flowers.

Use a round or long watermelon depending on what shape basket you want.

Experiment with the melon to decide how you want it to stand. Cut a very thin slice off the bottom so it will stand up.

Use a washable marking pen and mark a line all around the middle. Draw lines where you want the handle.

Make straight cuts down each side of the handle to the line you drew around the middle. Then make horizontal cuts from the middle line inward to connect with the cuts you made for the handle. Remove those sections and refrigerate for another use. Practice making a basket with a handle on a potato to understand the technique.

Carefully scoop out watermelon pulp from the basket with an ice cream scoop and refrigerate for another use.

You can cut zig-zags around cut edge of the basket for a nice finishing touch. Draw with a marking pen first.

After you have become accomplished at making watermelon baskets, you can experiment with carving some detail into the surface of the watermelon, such as a triangle pattern. Mark an even pattern across melon with criss crossed masking tape and cut out areas in between tape with an Exacto knife. Remove tape and see your nice even carving design.

Watermelon baskets can be prepared a day or two ahead of time. Wrap it in plastic wrap and refrigerate.

"Spiked" Watermelon

1 bottle (fifth or liter)   1 large watermelon
    vodka or white wine   ice

Cut a hole into the watermelon just large enough for the neck of the bottle to fit. Save the piece of watermelon to use as a plug. Place the watermelon in an ice chest and balance it upright with towels if necessary. Open the bottle and place it in the hole in the watermelon. When the bottle is empty replace the plug. Cover the watermelon with ice and let it sit overnight.

Watermelon Balls Deluxe

2 cups watermelon balls   1 cup blueberries
2 cups halved strawberries   1/2 cup sour cream
1 cup honeydew melon balls   1/2 cup powdered sugar
1 cup cantaloupe balls   1/2 cup orange juice

Combine fruit in large bowl. Combine remaining ingredients in small bowl. Mix. Pour sour cream mixture over fruit. Chill one hour or longer. Serves 6-8.

Mexican Watermelon

1 cup fresh lime juice   1/2 tsp. salt
1 tsp. tequila   1" watermelon cubes.
1/4 tsp. hot pepper sauce   chilled

Mix first 4 ingredients in a small bowl. With bamboo skewers, dip watermelon cubes into lime juice mixture.

Peach Sun Preserves

2 lbs. fresh ripe peaches   1/4 cup lemon juice
3 cups sugar

Peel peaches and discard pits. Cut into 1/2" thick slices. Measure 4 cups fruit and mix with the sugar and lemon juice in a large pan. Mix gently. Cover and let stand 1 hour.

Bring to a boil over medium heat, stirring constantly. Increase heat and boil, uncovered, for 4 minutes without stirring. Remove heat and let stand 30 minutes. Spread into a baking sheet with 1/2" to 3/4" sides (jelly roll pan). Cover with plastic wrap, leaving 1" uncovered along one side.

Place in direct sun. Stir gently every hour, turning fruit over. Leave in the sun 2 to 10 hours until fruit is plump and the juice is the consistency of corn syrup. If necessary, bring in at night and put back in the sun the next day.

Place in hot, dry, sterilized jars. Seal and store in refrigerator. These keep up to 4 weeks.

You can also make this with strawberries.

Peach Conserve

4 cups peeled and chopped   1/2 cup golden raisins
    peaches   7 cups sugar
1/4 cup lemon juice   1 cup finely chopped nuts
1 Tb. grated lemon rind   1/2 bottle Certo

Place all ingredients except nuts and Certo in a large pan. Bring to a boil over medium heat. Boil for 1 1/2 minutes. Remove from heat. Stir in nuts and Certo. Skim off foam, if necessary. Place hot conserve in hot, dry, sterilized jars. Seal and process in hot water bath or store in refrigerator.

Spiced Peaches

3 lb. medium fresh firm
  ripe peaches
12 whole cloves
4 1/2 cups sugar

3 cups cider vinegar
1 cinnamon stick, broken
  into 4 pieces and crushed
3/4 cup red hots candy

Drop peaches, 3 to 4 at a time, into a pot of boiling water and let them boil 2 to 3 minutes. With a slotted spoon, move peaches to a colander and rinse with cold water. Peel them with a small sharp knife. Push a whole clove into each peach and drop peaches into hot, dry, sterilized wide-mouthed canning jars.

In a large non-aluminum pan, bring sugar, vinegar, cinnamon and red hots to a boil over high heat, stirring until sugar dissolves. Ladle hot syrup over peaches, a little at a time, allowing it to run to the bottom of the jar before adding more.

Cover tightly with seals and rings. Cool to room temperature and refrigerate at least 3 days.

Peach Pound Cake

2 sticks butter, softened
3 cups sugar
6 eggs, room temperature
1 tsp. vanilla
1 tsp. almond extract
3 cups flour

1/4 tsp. baking soda
1/2 tsp. salt
1/2 cup sour cream
2 cups ripe peaches, peeled
  and chopped
whipped topping to serve

In a large bowl, cream butter and sugar with electric mixer. Add eggs, one at a time, beating well after each one. Blend in extracts. Place dry ingredients in a separate large bowl and blend with a whisk. Add dry ingredients to creamed ingredients. Mix until blended. Fold in sour cream and peaches. Pour into greased and floured tube pan. Bake at 350 for 1 1/4 to 1 1/2 hours or until a toothpick inserted in center comes out clean.

French Bachelor's Dessert
"Confiture de Vieux Garçon"

This is a summer long recipe. In the fall it rests until Christmas when it is brought out and served in dessert dishes or in coffee cups. The fruit loses its color and the liquid is a dark rich color.

fresh sweet cherries
   with stems
fresh strawberries, hulled
fresh raspberries
fresh apricots
fresh peaches

fresh nectarines
fresh plums
fresh figs
seedless green grapes
seedless red grapes
sugar
vodka or light rum

Use a one gallon stoneware container. Add each fruit in the order listed throughout the summer as they come into their peak. Do not add any citrus fruits or melons. To add fruits with pits, cut fruit in half and discard pit.

Each time you add a fruit, add an equal weight of sugar on top of fruit. DO NOT STIR. Add enough liquor to cover the fruit each time. Keep loosely covered. Add another fruit, an equal amount of sugar and top off with liquor. The sugar will weight down the fruit. DO NOT EVER STIR. Finish by mid September. Put on a tight lid. Place in a dark, cool place until Christmas.

Fruit Pizza

1 roll refrigerated sugar cookie dough	fresh strawberries, hulled and halved
1 (8 oz.) block cream cheese, softened	kiwi fruit, peeled, halved and sliced
1/3 cup powdered sugar	bananas, sliced
pineapple chunks	blueberries
fresh peaches, peeled, sliced	lemon juice

Cut cookie dough into 1/4" thick slices. Place slices on an ungreased pizza pan and bake at 350 for about 10 minutes or until lightly browned. Cool. Spread cream cheese over crust. Shake powdered sugar through a strainer over cream cheese. Toss banana slices and peaches with lemon juice. Arrange fruit over pizza. Choose any design you like. A good design is to start in the middle and make circles of fruit until the entire pizza is covered. Chill. Cut into wedges to serve.

Frosted Grapes

egg whites	sugar
seedless green grapes	

Beat egg whites with a whisk until frothy. Separate grapes into small bunches (6 grapes or so each). Dip grapes into beaten egg whites and roll in sugar. Dry on a cake rack. Chill. Serve as part of a tray of assorted fruits.

Colored Sugar

1 cup sugar	a few drops food coloring

Place sugar in a jar. Add food coloring. Put on lid and stir and shake until coloring is evenly mixed. Serve in hot or iced tea or coffee. Serve sprinkled on fresh fruit or hot cereal.

Index